ALESSANDRO NARDONE

TRUMP, ALEX AND ME

TRANSLATION BY MIRIAM MAZZA

Youcanprint *Self-Publishing*

Title | Trump, Alex and me
Author | Alessandro Nardone

ISBN | 978-88-92651-43-2

Youcanprint Self-Publishing
Via Roma, 73 - 73039 Tricase (LE) - Italy
www.youcanprint.it
info@youcanprint.it
Facebook: facebook.com/youcanprint.it
Twitter: twitter.com/youcanprintit

To all fools

INTRODUCTION

THE ELECTORAL campaign which ended on the night of 8th November was, in many ways, the most crazy and unpredictable of the whole American history. I defy anyone to say that on June 16th of one year ago, the day when Donald Trump announced his candidacy in the Republican primaries, no one would even bet a single dollar on the success of the New York tycoon. At that time no one believed it, neither I. Nevertheless, week after week, state after state, debate after debate, provocation after provocation, "The Donald" had the ability to deny all forecasts, not only winning the primaries, but even ridiculing the unfortunate Republican opponents. To put it in football slang, he threw them all a curve ball.

A child's play? Not at all, because to fully understand the capacity of the "Cyclone Trump", it is essential to contextualize his descent into the field, considering factors such as the candidacy of Jeb Bush that, it should be remembered, for his campaign could count on a much more conspicuous budget compared to the one scraped together from the powerful representative of another dynasty, that is Hillary Rodham Clinton. Unfortunately for him, the former governor of Florida was the best candidate at the worst moment. I say this due to the fact that Jeb has always represented the milder wing of the Grand Old Party, particularly in the field of immigration, and, excluding his surname, in a hypothetical battle with Hillary, he could have catalyzed around himself a very large slice of the democratic discontent with respect to the never really digested candidacy of Hillary. However, good Jeb had the misfortune to get two obstacles in his path that, soon, have become insurmountable: the first one was undoubtedly the great feeling of dissatisfaction with the establishment that was hatched for years mostly in the ashes of the middle class, and the second one, Donald Trump, which is simply the consequence of the first one. Thus, the would-third president of Bush house, former governor, moderate, husband of the Mexican Columba, after having quickly gained the favor of predictions, was obliged to cope with the impossible that gradually became reality, that is a candidate, his mirror image, who gave him a good hiding. An inevitable epilogue, also due to the blunders made by Bush himself and his staff, apparently frustrated by the fact that they had never been really in the game.

Regarding the other candidates, the only one able to provide Trump a few headaches, has been the ultraconservative Ted Cruz, not surprisingly he is also a supporter of very strong and sometimes extreme positions about fundamental issues such as the fight against immigration and the defense of the right to acquire and hold weapons sanctioned by the Second Amendment. Whereas, for Rubio, Kasich, Paul, Fiorina and Carson, the race for the nomination has been, euphemistically, very stingy with moments of glory.

As things settled down, it appears even more clear how that chain of events constituted the natural habitat for my performance in the shoes of another outsider, Alex Anderson, the fake candidate with whom, through the Net, I managed to have nearly 30,000 followers on Twitter receiving invitations to television and radio shows, and even in a public debate with the other candidates. A unique and extraordinary experience that allowed me to experience personally this election campaign, first measuring myself for about ten hours a day (or rather per night) with tens of thousands of Americans, many of whom part of the so-called "Deplorables" (Clinton called them in this way, making a huge mistake), that is, the people of Trump and subsequently, thanks to the intuition of the Director Luca Dini, in the role of Vanity Fair Italy reporter in Cleveland for the Republican Convention, and then in Philadelphia and New York during the elections, and Washington DC for the Inauguration Day. You will understand that for me, passionate about politics and in love with the US ever since I used to wear short trousers, it was like entering into the rabbit hole.

As I said at the end of my video reportage, which could only end at the White House, Alex was my pass to participate in dozens of side events at the Republican National Convention, where I were able to meet some of the protagonists of Donald Trump's ride, including VP Mike Pence and his campaign manager Kellyanne Conway, but also to attend extraordinary events such as the concert in which Bruce Springsteen and John Bon Jovi, along with Barack Obama, have closed the Hillary campaign in Philadelphia, in a charming location such as Independence Hall. Moreover Hillary invited me to follow the election night from the Javits Center press room in New York where, along with hundreds of journalists from all over the world, I have been able to comment on Hillary's defeat, even before the Trump's victory. Mainly for the monopoly that the Democratic candidate has exerted on endorsement and polls, that were all resoundingly wrong at the end.

To seal this journey of mine, along with my video reportage (that you can watch at this link: www.Americaisnow.com), I decided to realize this volume in which I intend to retrace the electoral campaign just ended through 18 articles and an analysis on Trump communications made by Francesco Fabiano, which all together, in a certain way, make up a fairly faithful mosaic of the facts that have taken place hitherto, certifying moreover, that would have been enough to go deeper into the internal dynamics of the two major parties, to get out of living rooms and to attend a little of "real America" in order to perceive that polls giving Clinton as a sure winner, were smelling a rat. Now that the spotlights of the election campaign went off, "The Donald" will have to prove himself and the whole world he has been underestimated twice: as candidate and as president.

Washington, Alessandro Nardone, bye bye.

I

HILLARY CLINTON, SHE IS THE WINNER
FOR ANTIPATHY AND SCANDALS
Il GiornaleOFF - April 19th, 2015

HILLARY is here. This is not a surprise. The story says clearly that Clinton is a candidate for the White House in real permanent service since the day she made her entrance into it as First Lady of her husband Bill. The fact is that we have witnessed, little surprised, the most announced announcement of all times, foundation stone of an objectively well-designed media campaign – considering Hillary's almost limitless budget – that could only be launched through a Tweet.

It is obvious that you speak ad write about a political-media event of this magnitude, don't mention it, but what is giving us some perplexity, are some comments which, in our latitudes, we got used to over the years. I mean the easy infatuations that many of our Italian *dem* are used to, accustomed to idealize the "foreign pope" on duty as the perfect man or woman, those who "would like be Americans just to be able to vote him," but then, quite often, they are forced to engage reverse gear in front of the evidence of the facts.

To support this trivial consideration of mine, excluding the countless examples that could be given, there are the moods of *dem* which are really called into question, the Americans, who are not exactly jumping for joy, for the second descent into the field of Clinton. Quite the contrary.

Yes, because if Hillary looks set to win the Democratic primary, with less of twists currently unreal (such an Obama endorsement in favor of another candidate maybe his Vice

Joe Biden), in Capitol Street they are fully aware of the fact that the former Secretary of State would be the best candidate to deal with, for the Republican opponents.

The reasons are different, ranging from Clinton family's skeletons in the cupboard, passing through the scandal (it has been talked so little about it in our country) triggered by such carelessness of Hillary, in the days when she was Secretary of State, when she was using her private mail server, putting at risk the privacy of US diplomacy; and for her gross errors as the slowness with which she managed the response to the American Embassy's attack in Benghazi, in which four American citizens lost their lives; and, still on the subject of Libya, her interventional line which destabilized the Country paving the way to Isis cutthroats.

Last but not least, the fact that Hillary is not exactly a great communicator and that, indeed, she very often appears even to be unpleasant; and this turned out to be decisive during the campaign of 2008, during which she collected lots of mistakes forcing her to raise the white flag, letting Barack Obama to be crowned. Aware of this and of the fact that she can certainly not stand as the newness because of her age and curriculum (if not only for a mere matter of gender), she strongly wanted Kristina Schake by her side, that is, the communications specialist who helped Michelle Obama at the White House, to become an icon of style and liking.

II

ALL THE TRUMP CARDS OF JEB BUSH
Il GiornaleOFF - June 18th, 2015

THEREFORE Jeb, runs. Of course, as in the case of Clinton, we are talking about an announced message but, unlike the Democratic candidate, the one on the horizon of the aspirant third president of the Bush Dynasty, will be true election campaign. Then, in all likelihood, the Republican nomination will be his, but he will have to earn it against candidates such as his former heir Marco Rubio and the recent winner of the parliamentary battle against NSA mass interception, the libertarian Rand Paul. The fact is that there are several factors playing in favor of the former governor of Florida, first of all the statistical ones: from 1952 up today, the GOP nomination has always been conquered by its leading candidates. In fact, Barry Goldwater, Richard Nixon, Ronald Reagan, Bush 41th, Robert Dole, Bush 43rd, John MacCain and Mitt Romney, have all announced their candidacy one year before the elections.

According to the data, a further consideration emerges, from which, most likely, we learn that the name of the next occupant of the White House will be out from the Republican primaries; not only thanks to the (many) thorns in Hillary Clinton side. Yes because, after a double mandate, Americans have very often chosen the opposition party: it happened in 1960, 1968, 1976, 2000 and in 2008. Ronald Reagan – but in this case, we talk about a true champion of American politics – as a result of the wide victory over Jimmy Carter in 1980, he succeeded in reversing this trend, laying the groundwork for the victory of his deputy in 1988, when a very large chunk of the electorate acted as if it was ready to vote the third term of Reagan and not the first one of George

Bush Senior.

It goes without saying that if Jeb Bush should run for the White House, besides marking distances from his father and his brother – as indeed has already shown willingness to do, starting with his logo that, as in his campaign for the position of Governor, consists in Jeb!, without any trace of his surname – he will have to succeed in shaking off from the GOP the obsession with finding a new Reagan, rather than reaffirming timeless ideas about federalism and power of the individual against the State. In short, the Republicans will have to stop talking about it and start acting like him, because this would be the way to regain the true heart of their electorate, that is, that middle class which was literally brought to its knees by static politics of Obama Administration.

It is true, very true indeed, about some positions (see immigration), Jeb Bush is judged too accomodating, especially by the most intransigent wing of the Republican electorate, but it must be noted that after having lost two presidential elections one after another, you tend to appoint more moderate candidates: Jimmy Carter has been more moderate of McGovern, Clinton of Dukakis and Bush of Dole.

In short, there are all the conditions for the victory of Jeb, with the support of historical data – which is always good – and with the consents he is taking advantage within the establishment of GOP; and if so it will be, then, it will witness a clash between dynastic candidates ready to do anything to become the forty-fifth President of the story, challenging each other in an electoral campaign that, in these terms, would have the strange taste of a movie remake.

III

DONALD TRUMP, A BERLUSCONI
WITHOUT A FACTION
Il GiornaleOFF - October 13rd, 2015

DONALD TRUMP is really the Berlusconi across the ocean? A sort of Stars and Stripes Knight? Absolutely yes, according to what is written by some authoritative commentators who, mostly, build their theory by arguing with fundamental issues such as boaster, nasty money, a thinly-veiled sexism and, that's incredible, «a troubled relationship with their hair». Really! So, if it is true that both feel some adversity for what is politically correct, it should also be noted that Berlusconi did not ran in the primaries of an existing party but, in just some weeks, he succeeded in three challenges in one go: founding a political entity which was ranked first immediately, putting together the coalition (or rather, coalitions) with which he won elections and, consequently, preventing the seizure of power by the post-communist left party.

From the electoral marketing point of view it was a real miracle, in which the former Knight was the capable man, for at least fifteen years, to snap around himself an impressive body of consensus, turning him into the absolute protagonist of the political scene, excluding successes and failures. We can not say the same about Trump, whose candidacy, more than a descent, seems to be an encroach on territory, and for many aspects it is extempoiraneous and ending unto itself.

So if Berlusconism exists, in part still resists, and in a few years will be judged by posterity, there is no trace of

Trumpism, jokes and slogans aside.

But we must recognize a great merit to the American builder, I mean that he laid bare the big limits of the current aspirants to the nomination of the GOP (Republican Party) for the presidential elections from which Obama's successor will be nominated. If Scott Walker and Rick Perry have abdicated even before beginning, Jeb, the third aspirant President at Bush home, seems to lack that berlusconian "something" that would enable him to make a breach in the heart of that Republican electorate which shows not to like, just to give an example, his "too accomodating" positions on illegal immigration.

On the other hand, despite his good performance in the last debate, the former CEO of Hewlett Packard Carly Fiorina, seems like to fight for the nomination as vice, rather than the final victory, with Carson, Cruz and Rubio. Yes, but vice to whom? In Washington, many people think that the real race for the Republican nomination will begin only after the eventual exit of Donald Trump as well as, among Democratics, many of them are looking forward that the current Vice President Joe Biden takes the field sweeping away, in one go, both Clinton and Sanders, two candidates who, for different reasons, have not been swallowed by the leaders of their party.

IV

Conflict Trump – Cruz:
That's Why the Crisis Also Affects
US Right Wing
Il Giornale d'Italia - February 2nd, 2016

It is true that Italian right wing is in poor condition, but it is also true that elsewhere even conservatives are not much better. Quite the contrary. This is the case of American Republicans and their own party – nicknamed GOP (which stands for Grand Old Party) – in which the atmosphere is not exciting at all, and stinks of resignation to the impending disaster. However, blaming the cyclone Trump would be superficial, as well as incorrect: rather, more than the cause, the New York-based tycoon is the effect of a laceration that has very deep roots, which sink in the arid soil of a land made up of divisions that are certainly political, but also cultural and religious, that you must know in order to better understand the dynamics that have led two persons as Cruz and Trump to reach the role of the main contenders for the nomination.

A bit of history, thus. At the end of the second mandate of Ronald Reagan, the Republican Party had several trends inside itself; among these, the most interesting ones for the purposes of our discussion, were basically two. We could call the first one the "liberals" trend, whose leader was certainly Barry Goldwater and that felt a strong sense of intolerance against President Reagan, to the point of preferring both Nixon and Ford. On the other hand, the second current was the "populist" one, a segment of a party that initially was dragged by Nixon and Eisenhower and then inherited by Reagan mainly for his ability to do politics "with his head held high", and being able to speak to the hearts of the Republican electorate making full use of the so-called "traditional values" of the stars and stripes Right.

The link between the two factions was the Cold War, whose end marked the reopening of the internal conflict. We are talking about movements which in some cases were also carriers of a healthy cultural ferment, as well as elements of genuine political innovation, as the Gingrich revolution in the '90s and the birth, during the first years of this decade, of independent clubs known as the Tea Party, able to characterize what we might define as "the (spasmodic) research of the perfect conservative", which began with the primaries of 2010, marked by the triumph of several candidates coming from the ranks of this trend.

Since then, into GOP a race has started in order to gain the primacy of "the most Republican" which, besides supporting a quick encroachment of the party line towards populist tendencies, has also marked it from a legislative point of view. In fact, despite having obtained the majority at the Congress, the Grand Old Party has almost quit its role as ruling national party because of an opposition which, instead of causing difficulties to the Obama administration, has even ended up by promoting it. Many slogans, few facts, or rather none. Not to mention the confusion of the political offer, I mean the program: about fundamental issues such as immigration, Cruz and Trump say something, while Jeb Bush and his former heir Marco Rubio say something else.

What emerges from this mess is that, after having been close to 52% of the vote in Iowa, according to polls, the struggle for gaining delegates of other states, it will remain prerogative of Cruz and Trump, even if all the other candidates of the Party would form a coalition with each other by converging their votes onto a single competitor (Rubio?).

The mixture of all these elements produced the result that Trump drew strength also and above all from the attacks coming from the Republican establishment because, first of all, they were addressed to an electorate that, initially, was not keen to vote for him. As well as all critics to his excessive cockiness and his abhorrence for political correct have had no dissuasive effect on his supporters who, rather, felt it as to be a snobbish outrage of media and political elites, considered to be so distant from what they consider the real common sense of the American "hard and pure" Right.

I am sure that these Republicans leaders will play any card in order to prevent Trump to win the nomination, becoming the very probable defeated in the presidential elections on November 8. Including seeking an agreement with Cruz although he is unpopular with almost all the party. On the other hand, in the headquarters of the New York tycoon, someone will certainly be convinced by the fact that it is not a coincidence that, in English, "winning cards" becomes "trump cards". All we can do is to wait that everyone makes his move, but we also have a certainty: nothing in the GOP, after the "Cyclone Trump", will be the same.

V

THE MASSACRE IN ORLANDO AND TREACHEROUS DICTATORSHIP OF DEMAGOGY

Il GiornaleOFF - June 13th, 2016

As SOME of you probably know, some weeks ago I raised hell by telling BBC about my "candidacy" to the White House through an alter ego - Alex Anderson - who was no one but the main character of my latest novel.

Well, if he had really existed, after the terrible extermination of Orlando, Alex would have done three things, without thinking too much about it: to begin with, he would have suspended the election campaign as a sign of respect for the victims, their families and the gay community, because is not correct to make propaganda on the backs of recent dead people. The next moment he would have phoned President Obama, guaranteeing him closeness and support and, finally, he would have granted a declaration in support of President and any initiative aimed at introducing stricter rules on the purchase and possession of weapons.

Even in this tragic circumstance, the character of Alex Anderson is useful to mark the differences between what the American political offer currently has – Hillary and Trump – and what it would be desirable, but which, unfortunately, is simply the result of the imagination of many Americans who do not feel themselves well represented neither from one nor from the other one.

So, if I had to give a title to the flood of declarations rained during these hours, it would definitely be *Show must go on, because, not only it did not come to anyone mind to bury the hatchet for a few hours but*, on the contrary, everyone raised the tone: on one side, Trump predictably dived immediately into the mud of speculation, and on the other side Clinton immediately followed him, instead of letting him go.

That being said, I think is necessary to make some reflection on what happened.

About the issue of weapons: it is a veritable Moloch for many Democrats (even Sanders voted against stricter rules) and nearly all Republicans who, over the decades, have built up substantial portions of their own consensus on the defense of the Second Amendment. Needless to say, rather than an actual matter of principle, for them it is a duty towards the gun lobby (see NRA), which is keeping them under control, after having them generously supported, as well as voted. It seems paradoxical that the country, which in many ways is actually "the greatest western democracy", allows anyone to get hold of every kind of weapons with the same ease with which you buy a kilo of bananas but then, paradox to the paradox, it exposes the entire population to the NSA mass interceptions (see under Edward Snowden), however with poor results, considering that Omar Mateen, the author of the massacre, he has been under FBI control for several month, but then FBI decided to slacken him off. That is to say that even the "Orwellian Big Brother" of the National Security Agency can really do little for the prevention of crimes committed by splinter group, like the one in Orlando.

It would be necessary something like the Precrime of Minority Report, but, until we wait for someone who will succeed in inventing it seriously, we might begin with something apparently banal, that is, to prevent anyone who can get hold of weapons, especially crazy men already known by the Police.

The massacre has an advantage for Trump: as it is

known, the propaganda of the Republican front runner is so often demagogical, also and above all with regard to immigration and the fight against Islamic terrorism. The wall on the border with Mexico, and the closure of borders for Muslims are his most famous slams, but certainly not the only ones. It would be enough to attend one of his meetings to understand that all his electoral campaign is orchestrated not on concrete proposals, but on slogans, jokes of questionable taste and unrealistic slogans. It is obvious, from his point of view, tweet a sentence as «I told you so». I am so sure that, if you have followed the fourth series of House of Cards, you would have certainly linked the end of the last episode (in which the two Underwood try to overshadow a journalistic inquiry that had just overwhelmed them, due to to the execution of an American hostage by Islamic fundamentalists) with the tactic of Trump which, excluding extremisms due to the fact that in the first case it is simply fiction, is the same as the one adopted by Frank Underwood.

Act of terror and hate or attack of Islamic matrix: at the moment I think it's objectively useless to strive over form, also because the substance says that the criminal who killed fifty people at Pulse in Orlando, was born and grew in the United States where, in addition, was working as a security officer. Therefore I suppose it is highly unlikely to think of a real contiguity between them and the ISIS, rather I believe that Omar Mateen in some way represents the new frontier of Islamic terrorism, the less controllable one, precisely because it is not organic in any organization or cell, composed of individuals born and grown in the West that, at some point in their lives, decide to join the criminogenic cause of the Islamic state. What is certain is that, both criminal records of the killer and delirious proclamations of his father complete a disturbing picture, without forgetting the investigations to which they were subjected by the FBI. «He was known to police»: how many times have we read or heard this phrase? Practically always, if we think about attacks in Paris and in Brussels, and partly also in San

Bernardino. This is to say that it is misleading to say that a similar phenomenon can be fought by closing borders, while it is plausible to think that it should be done strongly reaffirming Western values, by awakening the conscience of peoples who, since longtime, have been eradicated of their roots and have lost landmarks, role models, trustable guides. From the remotest suburban school, up to the highest backbenches in parliament.

In conclusion, going back to the American match, I am convinced this is the historical moment in which the Republicans can and must transform their daemon Trump from threat into opportunity, by treating him the same way as a *bad company* to whom leave vulgar tones, racist propaganda and an objectively indefensible defense of principles such as free trade in arms. Will they lose the election? Oh well, anyway the winner would be Trump, not them. We might as well lay the foundation for building a new longer-term perspective, rather than resign ourselves to the dictatorship of demagogy. It can happen that, maybe, in four years, they will have a real Alex Anderson to support, with conviction.

VI

DO YOU REMEMBER ALEX ANDERSON? WE SENT HIM TO TRUMP
by Vanity Fair - July 23rd, 2016

HIS NAME is Alessandro Nardone, 40 years old, coming from Lake Como and he made a big mess in America for eight months. Equipped with a pair of dark Ray-Ban and a charming smile, with an institutional website and tempting slogans, he passed off as Alex Anderson, the Republican candidate for the White House, ready to challenge Donald Trump and Hillary Clinton.

His story, discovered by BBC and told by Vanity Fair, began in June last year. Alessandro, marketing consultant, is about to launch his third book in the US. The title is The Predestined. The story is about Alex Anderson, a young member of the US Congress chased by a former CIA agent. Alessandro wants to promote his book. But, since «he did not have a red cent», he decides to bring Alex Anderson to life, at least online.

In June, in Como, he registers the domain Alexanderson2016.com, while in Washington Democrats and Republican candidates are warming themselves up for the primaries. On that baroque site in red and blue colors, he writes the biography of Alex. «Born in 1976 in Los Angeles, after his graduation at Yale and after having worked as a prosecutor, in 2012 he was re-elected to Congress in the District of California».

He proposes his program («Less taxes for all»), his codewords («Job, opportunity, change») and his slogan («America is now»), completing it with the omnipresent Stars and Stripes. His masterpiece is the video on which he communicates his descent into the field to Americans. He promotes himself on socials, with a special *itanglish*. A perfect balance of rock music, filters in Instagram style and superimposed hashtags. Quickly he is taken seriously. Alex Anderson website records nearly 200,000 visits. And his Twitter account gets almost 30,000 followers.

In February, however, after a triumphal campaign, he is discovered by the BBC. On that experience, Alessandro wrote a book, «Yes web can». We sent him to Cleveland, to the Republican convention in which Donald Trump has accepted the nomination for the race for the White House.

VII

AND SENATOR TOLD ME:
«ALEX, LET'S MAKE A SELFIE»
Vanity Fair - July 27th, 2016

Cleveland, July 21

«THE WEST SIDE belongs to whites and the East Side belongs to blacks: is a deeply divided city, like all America. Obama tried to change things, but he found too much oppositions. Moreover this is a country born and raised on slavery, not on equality ».

Welcome back to reality. On the way back to the hotel, the words which Jackie – a classy black man of sixty who on evenings makes up his wages by doing the Uber driver on his Lexus – told me, are worth a thousand analysis on the discourse with which Donald Trump has just agreed, in the Quicken Loans Arena, his nomination as Republican candidate. Because his words explain this America, or rather *these Americas*, much more than the slogans heard at the Republican Convention, slogans that have never been so low in political contents.

Forget the oceanic demonstrations of the past. Cleveland – a quiet town in Ohio emptied of its identity, transformed for four days into a «non-place» – is the paradigm of the mutation which, in the era of social media, digs a deeper and deeper gap between appearance and substance. Once, with less space and more time available, journalists used to select, and barely would have taken care of the anything that has happened here. But nowadays everything is «twittered», pre-chewed to fill an article, a photo, a television reportage at once. If each of us is a potential media, the masses are not needed any more. It is enough a tiny group of demonstrators, two placards handwritten with a marker: the operators of information scattered around the city – 20 thousand – are ready to give anyone his 15 minutes of fame. And Donald Trump won, precisely thanks to this process of «making things twittered»: communicating not concrete proposals but simple (and often trivial) slogan. Behind the tweet there is nothing.

Only in such a context, an Italian like me, Alessandro Nardone, could have kept alive for several months – with my pseudonym Alex Anderson – a «fake» campaign for the Republican nomination, without arousing suspicion neither in my tens of thousands of followers on Twitter nor among experts, who kept on inviting me to their interviews and broadcasts. On the contrary, my horizontal communication strategy – answering every message personally, not like all the others who gave the management of their social profiles in the hands of highly paid teams – made me feel more real than the real candidates.

Only in March, during the Super Tuesday, I did come out on the BBC, and the news of the fake candidate appeared on the media all over the world. But to catapult Alex Anderson for the first time into the real world of interactions was Vanity Fair, that sent me here, in Cleveland, to write the reportage you are reading.
But let's start from the beginning.

July, 17

After landed, I give myself a few hours of rest. Then I wear Alex T-shirt and I reach the Quicken Loans Arena, where everything is ready for tomorrow's Convention. I sit on the Public Square bleachers, watching the sun rising behind the Cuyahoga County Soldiers' and Sailors' Monument. What a surprise: a group of delegates recognizes me, stops me and asks for a selfie. The first of a long series of selfie with young militants, but also with Congressional representatives and Senators. Real politicians who want to take a photo with this fake candidate. Around the Arena, a market is taking shape whose stands are selling all sorts of Trump gadgets: t-shirts, hats, pins, puppets with swaying head, packs of corn flakes, even condoms. There are crowds of people, and an impressive number of police officers controlling the area. The images of tragic attacks in Europe are still impressed in everybody eyes, morever here fierce protests of the opposing factions, free to manifest armed, are expected.

July, 18

Galen, the cameraman, comes and picks me up. You can feel a lot of tension everywhere. Cops are everywhere: on foot, on horseback, on mountain bikes specially purchased by the local administration. There is talk of 5,500 agents, of which 3000 federal and 2000 "imported" from other States.

Elbowing in the crowd – with plenty of journalists – we reach the head of a procession of Black Lives Matter movement: «Whites kill us like dogs, and no one does anything», a boy shouts in my microphone.

Not far, a dozen of Pro-Guns are parading, with Kalashnikovs on their shoulders, magazines and bulletproof vests. I see that one of them has the written «We the People» tattooed on the forearm, first three words of the Preamble of the US Constitution which includes the Second Amendment too, the one that guarantees the right to own weapons that, along with the hate for taxes and the invasiveness of the government, represents the Republican paradigm par excellence. «If China had had the Second Amendment, the communist regime would never have taken power», one of them tells me. «Weapons, as well as self-defense, are a democratic guarantee».

As soon as the Convention begins, the protests become less noisy every day, thanks to the wise attitude of the police, which controls and contains everything, without allowing nervousness.

The CBS television network and the prestigious political monthly *The Atlantic* invite me to their in-depth discussions between journalists and members of the party. I ask Chris Wilson, campaign manager of the former favorite Ted Cruz, if other former rivals for the nomination – Romney, McCain, Bush, Rubio – were not wrong deserting the Convention, leaving room for an even more «berlusconized» Trump in his campaign of party personalization. The comparison with Berlusconi fits perfectly. Of course, they were wrong. Instead of staying at home, they should have come here and challenge him.

Not only the country and the city are split, but also a party that, in order to convince itself about the goodness of a nomination, brings out the comparison with Reagan. It is not a good comparison, because Ronald founded his victory on optimism. In this case, it's fears, troubled like ghosts, to have given the nomination to Donald Trump, ready to transform the White House into the set of his new, very personal reality show. *God Bless America.*

VIII

Donald Trump
from A to Z
Il Giornale - August 21st, 2016

A – The Art of the Deal:

The book, published in 1987, which became a real must for aspiring or successful businessmen, is the biography of Donald Trump, written with his *ghostwriter* Tony Schwartz; this sentence will be particularly useful to understand many of his comments: «Good advertising is surely preferable to the bad one but, on closer view, bad publicity is much better than no advertising at all. To clarify, polemics always promote». A few months ago "The Art of the Deal" also became a (satirical) movie in which Trump is played by Johnny Deep. Realized by Funny or Die, the video begins with the introduction of Ron Howard, who says he found a videotape of the eighties containing the film, which is now hard to find.

B – Berlusconi, Silvio:

«He is a businessman, he knows the economy better than anyone else», «He does not need politics to make money», «He will be successful in politics as in his enterprises», these sentences remind you of something, right? Of course you do, these are some of the strong points used by Silvio Berlusconi supporters since his "descent into the field", but also by most of Trump followers. But I was so amazed to find that, among US observers and professionals I met, almost no one has deepened the similarities between the New York tycoon and former Knight. Is it an excess of what we would call Americancentrism? It can be, but the fact is that it is enough to give them some examples in order to let them realize that there are so many similarities between the two, as well as not a few differences.

C – Cleveland:

The city in which, from 18th to 21st July, took place the Republican National Convention that gave Trump the scepter of Republican candidate in the presidential elections scheduled on November 8th. Actually, rather than inside Quicken Loans Arena, the real show took place on the streets of the city, literally invaded by a multitude of delegates, journalists, supporters and protesters. Moreover he was very good at putting into practice his plan of personalize the event (another similarity with Silvio), turning it into a sort of "Trump-Pride", forcing even the less enthusiastic Republicans (euphemism) of his candidacy, to bear him.

D – De Niro, Robert:

«Trump? He is completely nuts, like Travis Bickle in "Taxi Driver"». So Robert De Niro said during the fortieth anniversary of Martin Scorsese's masterpiece, harshly criticizing the candidacy of Trump comparing it to the main character of the movie.

E – Eastwood, Clint:

This time, the unforgettable Dirty Harry has no criminal in his gunsights, but political correctness: «Secretly everyone is getting tired of them. We are truly a generation of wuss». Along with the desire to break with the Obama administration, it is basically the absence of filters in the language of Trump, to have convinced the dean of Hollywood to choose him, «although I do not always agree with him».

F – First Lady (Melania):

In the beginning, there has been the evident plagiarism of the speech given by Michelle Obama in Denver during the Democratic convention of 2008, then doubts about her degree in architecture and consequent (lightning quick) removal of her website, and now the voices raised by

Politico.com on the alleged lack of requisites to work in the United States between '95 and '96, to which the aspiring First Lady replied with a tweet: «I have always been in compliance with the immigration laws of this country».

G – GOP:

It's the acronym for Grand Old Party. The Republican Party is likely to implode under the blows of Donald Trump, who does not avoid any occasion to attack the leaders – the so-called establishment – who, on their side, must consider sand in their pants infinitely less annoying compared to the New York tycoon. It must be said, however, that the outcome of the primary comes more from the (huge) mistakes of the party rather than the merits of Trump. In fact, in the 8 years of Obama administration, the party failed to characterize itself by any successful initiative, as well resulting insubstantial from the point of view of its representatives to Congress and to Senate. Just consider that Ted Cruz is a "maverick", perhaps the most disliked by the party of Trump, and that Marco Rubio is among the most ineffective politicians in Senate.

H – Hayden, Michael:

The former director of National Security Agency has signed, along with about fifty Republican experts on security (one of them is John Negroponte, the deputy of Condoleezza Rice), a letter in which they state they will not vote for Trump, although they do not even support Hillary Clinton; and even Hayden, by the CNN studios, did not hesitate to define it: «A big danger for the present and for the future».

I – Internet:

Despite his (not always appropriate) performances on Twitter seem to witness a passion for the Web, last December, a few days after the massacre in San Bernardino, during a meeting in South Carolina, Trump has referred to Bill Gates, wishing for a meeting with him and with «who really understands what's going on» in order to discuss the idea «of closing Internet and social medias in order to contain the spread of online extremists».

K – Khan, Khizr and Ghazala:

They are the parents of Captain Humayun Khan, the American muslim soldier killed in Iraq in 2004, and target of Trump's messy invectives for having supported the candidacy of Hillary from the stage of the Democratic convention in Philadelphia: «The manner in which he has been disrespectful to the mother of a killed soldier says a lot – the father of the soldier said – about a candidate President, unable to understand people of whom he would like to be the leader».

L – Lewandowsky, Corey:

Until a few weeks ago, he was the campaign manager of Trump, and widely defended him even when he was denounced and arrested on suspicion of having beaten Michelle Fields, a journalist for Breitbart News, in order to "dissuade her" from asking the candidate a very uncomfortable question. From his corner, Lewandowsky immediately declared his innocence, talking about «irrational» accusations. The fact is that, on June 21st, Trump has decided to fire him (it is said because of his family pressure, Ivanka first of all) and that Paul Manafort, who in the meantime had replaced Lewandowsky, on August 20th, has resigned after being accused of having received 13 "undeclared" million dollars from pro-Russian Ukrainian movements. Now, in a strange twist of fate, it has come the turn of Steve Bannon, former director of Breitbart, the site where Michelle Fields used to write.

M – Maples, Marla:

Model, actress and second wife of Donald Trump. A famous anecdote tells how, in '92, when Trump was on the brink of bankruptcy having fallen into debt for nearly $ 1 billion, just walking with her along the streets of Manhattan, he pointed to a homeless man lying on the roadside, and he told her:

«You see that bum? It has $ 900 million more than me».

N – Nixon, Richard:

Slogan aside, rather than Ronald Reagan (to whom, as you will read soon, his supporters are trying to approach), Donald Trump reminds us of Richard Nixon of "law and order", but also of the frenzied attacks to the media. In this regard, in his book on the tensions between the Nixon administration and journalism, James Goodale, a Times reporter, tells that: «Many of the journalists who dealt with of those elections, used to feel themselves in danger for what they wrote».

O – Ohio:

But also Florida, Pennsylvania and North Carolina: according to projections of the New York Times, Trump will necessarily have to conquer the "swing" States, in order to beat Hillary Clinton.

P – Pro Guns:

They are the strongest supporters of untouchability of the Second Amendment, that is, the part of the US Constitution which guarantees the right to own and bear weapons. During the Republican Convention, many of them marched through the streets of Cleveland with their weapons and, last August 10th, Trump invoked them directly by stating that «they might stop Hillary Clinton».

R – Reagan, Ronald:

We may easily say that Ronnie is the Republicans, as Berlinguer was the PCI and Almirante the MSI. It is indeed his name that was mentioned to snatch a sure applause or to warm the coldest hearts toward Trump; everyone, from his Vice candidate Mike Pence, try to legitimize Trump precisely through this (very forced) comparison with the president that marked an era thanks to his Reaganomics, but also and above all to his concept of optimism.

S – The Simpsons:

In "Bart to the future", an episode of The Simpsons broadcast in 2000, America is imagined in 2030 with Lisa –Bart's sister – who has become *"The first female heterosexual President of the United States" who, she explains to her staff, must first restore the income statements of the Country because: «as you know, we inherited a fairly critical budget by the President Trump». More recently, the characters by Matt Groening have targeted the Republican candidate, with Homer bending himself to the threats of Marge saying that he will give his vote to Hillary, sighing:* «here it is how I became democratic».

T – Taxes:

He says he wants to reduce them and give rise to «greater fiscal revolution since Reagan». What a pity that, unlike Hillary and his deputy Mike Pence, Trump insists on not wanting to divulge his income tax return.

U – Univision:

The very popular American network in Spanish language, whose most famous journalist, Jorge Ramos, during a press conference, has engaged a duel with Trump no holds barred on immigration, irritating him to the point to get rid of him with a disdainful: «Go back to Univision».

V – Viral:

It is the marketing concept on which Trump has relied since the beginning, first of all in order to compensate for the shortage of donations for his electoral campaign. During the Primaries, when *monstre* budgets like that of Jeb Bush (who had collected even more than Hillary Clinton) and lack of experience seemed an insuperable limit, he rather managed to bend them to his favor, forging a "Renzi style" campaign, positioning himself as an alternative to the old tools of the Republican establishment. The result was that he gave a diversification with his daily tough hits, gaining an infinitely greater media exposure than his competitors, thanks to which he loyalized veritable "people" that, in fact, always rush to his public events. And vote him.

W – The Wall:

It is not that of Pink Floyd and not even the one in Berlin, but it's the wall along the Mexican border that has become one of his most popular refrains. At his meetings, in all his speeches, Trump has always uttered the sentence: «We need to build a wall».

Z –Zio (Uncle) Sam:

Exonerated 5 times from military duty, Donald Trump managed to avoid the *I want you* of Uncle Sam to Vietnam through a medical certificate diagnosing «a thorn in his heel». However 47 years later, it was Vietnam to go to him, attacking a real Republican symbol such as John McCain, saying that: «He is a war hero because he was caught. In my opinion, he is not a hero, I prefer people who manage to not be caught». McCain's answer came just a few weeks ago, after Trump attacked the family of Captain Khan, with a concise: «I hope that the Americans understand that Trump comments do not represent the positions of the Republican Party».

IX

TV DEBATE TRUMP – CLINTON:
OR THE CHALLENGE OF THE TWO MOST
UNPOPULAR CANDIDATES
Vanity Fair - September 27th, 2016

IS IT a case that the most anticipated debate of all time saw the two most unpopular candidates in the history of US presidential elections facing each other? Absolutely not, because the sense of uncertainty and the desire to understand, created an expectation as to push America to pause and watch the duel that has been consumed tonight at Hofstra University in New York. The two candidates were perfectly aware of it, in fact, certainly not by chance, they immediately showed their intentions wearing each other's colors: blue tie for Donald Trump, and red dress for Hillary Clinton (at her 35th presidential debate). Not mere aesthetic choices, but dictated by precise rules of communication.

Red «strength and courage» for Hillary, and light blue «calm and dialogue» for Trump. In short, if the Democratic candidate, after pneumonia, needed to reveal her strength, the New York tycoon had to prove to possess the necessary equilibrium to perform the most important position of the Planet. Since the very beginning, we saw the fruits of the preparatory work carried out in recent weeks by Hillary Clinton, who simulated some debates with real dobles for Trump, as with Philippe Reines, the consultant for political strategies, known for his volcanic personality that closely resembles that of the Republican candidate. From his point of view, Donald Trump – who preferred to practice with a long session of questions under the supervision of the former mayor of the Big Apple, Rudy Giuliani – he immediately spoke to his opponent calling her «Secretary», a tactic to strengthen the main theme of his campaign, or presenting himself as the «new» against Hillary Clinton who, rather, is the establishment, the «disastrous» Obama administration, the failures in foreign affairs and the scandal of her emails.

Despite a lot of tactics, the first fight between the two candidates for the White House was anything but boring, I would rather say that we have certainly witnessed one of the most fought debates, sometimes even fiercely, of all times. Yes, because from both sides, the attitude was right away not to save blows to the opponent, with the clear prevalence of Donald Trump who pressed Clinton just on what she considers a point of strength, the experience, «You have not done anything in the last 30 years, how do you plan to do it now?», and about security «She wants to fight Isis and says she is looking on her website ...».

On the other hand, Hillary was very clever to defend herself when Trump has reproached her about the Emailgate, moving the discussion on Achilles' heel of her opponent, that is taxes. «Maybe Americans want to know if Trump has not paid taxes. Not to pay them, means not to give money to schools and to our soldiers. There are such conflicts of interest. About emails I made a mistake, there's no excuse, I am responsible for it». For the rest, usual effective Trump has emerged essentially, thanks to reassuring slogans like «law and order», and a fierce Hillary Clinton, very competent, but perhaps not very inclined to use a language that can reach the listener. Form and substance, in short. The ideal would be to find that synthesis which, unfortunately for the Americans (and not only), is just missing.

X

I TELL YOU ABOUT MIKE PENCE, THE DEPUTY CANDIDATE THAT REPUBLICANS PREFER TO TRUMP
PoliticManager.com - October 5th, 2016

ON THE American side, the man of the day is certainly Mike Pence. In fact, the governor of Indiana and candidate deputy to Trump, has made analysts and experts agree on his victory in the debate which was staged Tuesday night, in which he clearly prevailed on the running mate of Hillary Clinton, Tim Kaine.

I managed to meet Pence last July 19th in Cleveland, during a closed-door meeting organized by the American Conservative Union Foundation, a powerful Republican organization close to the NRA. On that occasion I saw in Pence a politician with an excellent oratorical skills, able to warm the hearts of an obviously unenthusiastic audience about the nomination just obtained by Donald Trump.

«On internet you will find one of my old picture, in which probably I was the same age as my son today, portraying me with President Reagan – he started saying in his speech – I knew Reagan, I know the man Trump and I know his heart. And trust me when I say he reminds me Ronald Reagan».

Then Pence went on defining Trump «a builder and a fighter, a father and a patriot. He will be a great president of the United States of America, because his heart beats with the heart of the American people». Despite the proximity to his great rival Ted Cruz, Trump has chosen Pence as his ticket companion in preference to iron Republican Newt Gingrich, according to many people this is a further step towards the unity of the party, taking advantage of his popularity among conservative voters, especially among those who supported other candidates during the battle no holds barred of the Republican primary elections.

Paradoxically, Republicans are united by an aversion they have for Hillary Clinton, rather than supporting Trump: it goes without saying that, in the conservative imagination, even more after the excellent performance on Tuesday night, the ideal candidate would be just Pence, and not the crazy variable Trump.

«His name should stand at the top of the ticket» the strategist of Pennsylvania Charlie Gerow said in Politico, while according to Michael Caputo, a former staff member of the New York tycoon campaign «Trump should get help from Pence in order to get ready for the next two debates with Hillary».

XI

TRUMP AND HILLARY,
THE MOST MISERABLE DEBATE
Vanity Fair - October 10th, 2016

A PAGE of history, probably the blackest of the contemporary American presidential campaigns. It started without the proverbial handshake between the two contenders, and ended with a feeble fair play beat induced by the last question, the debate went on stage last night in St. Louis has shown once and for all the very considerable limits of two candidates who divide (actually it should unite) drawing strength from each other's weak points. The shapes of Hillary Clinton and Donald Trump silhouetted on the background of the scandal of Trump Tapes, to which the Republican front runner answered in advance by calling a press conference focused on the alleged sexual harassments committed by Bill Clinton to Juanita Broaddrick, Paula Jones, Kathleen Willey and Kathy Shelton and forcing, in fact, his opponent to throw the ball into the stands dismissing the subject with a sharp «many of the things you say are not true», after having began by saying that «I disagreed with other Republican candidates, but I never said they could not be presidents. With Trump it is different. He says that the video does not represents him, but instead it is exactly what he is».

From his point of view, a visibly tired Donald Trump, answered the cheap shot of the Democratic candidate defining her squalid sexist sentences pronounced in 2005 as «speeches from the locker room, just words», while «those of Bill Clinton were actions: no one has ever abused women like him in the history of politics, he received the impeachment for sexual harassments» and then he shifted the focus on email-gate: «Hillary Clinton should be ashamed of herself and should apologize for the 33,000 emails she deleted», piling it on and accepting the commitment «if I become president» to appoint «a special prosecutor to investigate about you. You should go to jail».

With the passing of the minutes, the task of the excellent moderators Anderson Cooper and Martha Raddatz has not became easier at all, because the two candidates gave each other a good hiding even on apparently less hot topics compared to scandals such as economy, foreign and environmental policy. The reason lies in the choice that both Hillary and Trump has been carried out by, namely the customization of any topic. An approach that, speaking of taxes, has led to debate of the very heavy tax deductions of which even Trump confirmed he had benefited, stating however, to have done it «with your friends who are financing your electoral campaign», as well as, at the center of the debate on foreign affairs they ended up with mutual accusations such as «disasters made by you and Obama administration in the Middle East» said by Trump, or the reference to «business you are doing with Russia» raised by Hillary.

In short, a battle with no holds barred which undoubtedly helped Trump to keep on running for the Republican nomination, to strengthen his hard core and to try proselytizing in that big slice of the American electorate that still does not digest the candidacy of Clinton – including supporters of Sanders who, not surprisingly, he has nominated several times – and the Democratic candidate, to continue in his attempt to strengthen the idea of being the only plausible solution in a bid to thwart the dangers to which a unsuitable president as his opponent, would expose the country.

Variables and possible twists and turns of this crazy

electoral campaign are so numerous as to make any prediction just a mere supposition, but one thing is sure, namely that Americans, and with them every single citizen of the world, deserve much, much better than this worst.

XII

TRUMP WILL DECIDE «AT THE TIME» AND, LIKE HIM, MILLIONS OF AMERICANS
Vanity Fair - October 21st, 2016

THE BEST debate among the worst candidates. This, in essence, is the summary of the last of the three meetings between Hillary Clinton and Donald Trump went on stage last night at Univeristy of Nevada in Las Vegas, where both contenders were pressed on concrete issues by the excellent moderator Chris Wallace, famous face of Fox News.

That's right, because the truth is that the vast majority of Americans lives this electoral campaign going through the fact of having to choose between the two most unpopular candidates who, not surprisingly, took advantage of this debate in order to put together the fragments of their electorates.

On one side Hillary Clinton, whose history, both personal and political is poorly digested by a huge segment of the Dem world, up to the point to have paved the way for the real exploits of his opponent in the primaries, Bernie Sanders, first overtly socialist politician capable of conquering a so large consensus in the US. During the campaign for winning the nomination, both of them have inflicted each other severe blows, to the point that most of the supporters of Bernie today openly states they will vote for Trump just to be anti-Hillary. Well, it is certainly not a coincidence that last night Mrs Clinton has repeatedly articulated some of the keywords of the Sanders campaign such as when, for example, she began by stating that the Supreme Court «will have to stand on the side of minorities, not of banks and corporations».

On the other side there's Donald Trump, who won hands down the Republican primaries by cleverly insinuating himself between the cracks of a party torn by personal ambitions, also and above all thanks to his communicative unscrupulousness which, along with the lack of a credible opponent, allowed him to get fill of anti-establishment votes. This, however, does not mean he has conquered the majority of Republicans, on the contrary. He has simply led them to abstain. Thus, specularly to his greatest rival, he took advantage of the last chance at his disposal in an effort to recover a portion of that conservative electorate that perceives him as an intruder, defending tooth and nails the right of having weapons established by the Second Amendment of the US Constitution saying he was «proud of the support of NRA», inveighing against abortion and repeating his intention to build the wall on the border with Mexico because «we need it to stop the lords of drug».

Besides shoring up their respective electorates, the two main characters of the debate have given each other a good hiding even on matters such as eligibility to hold the position of President of the USA. «I will decide at the time whether to accept the result of the vote» is Trump (heavy) affirmation to which Hillary responded promptly «you reject everything that is not like how you want it», only to be told that elections «are rigged because you have committed serious crimes and you should not even be a candidate».

With regard to foreign policy, it was inevitable the reference to Vladimir Putin and (hard) relationship with Russia which, according to Clinton, has put in place an operation of unprecedented espionage «in order to determine the outcome of these elections», obviously in favor of Trump who, on his side, has replied by saying that she and Obama attack the Russian president «because he has proved to be smarter than you», but later he said he does not know him but if America and Russia will get along with each other «it will be a good thing».

There were also their Achilles heels, namely the trivial statements about women and the omission of tax return for Trump, the Emailgate and the Clinton Foundation for Hilary: uncomfortable facts, that they both have tried to dodge with sudden, as well messy, changes of subjects.

A debate which has not been won by anyone but which, in all probability, was lost by Trump, because he will be remembered for his «I will decide at the time» that, however, is exactly what many Americans will do when they go to vote.

XIII

TRUMP OVERTAKES HILLARY
AND AIMS TO THE WHITE HOUSE
Vanity Fair - November 2nd, 2016

IMAGINE Obama calling a press conference and, addressing the cameras as only he can do, he announces that «it was all a joke» because «we wanted to raise public awareness on the importance of these elections. Now the real electoral campaign begins with real candidates!». Raise your hand if you would give a sigh of relief. But it is not like that: unless a landing of aliens as in *Indipendence Day*, in exactly six days, Americans (in 20 million have already voted) will go to the polls to choose who, between Hillary Clinton and Donald Trump, at noon on the next January 20th will be officially the forty-fifth president of the United States of America.

Meanwhile, for the first time since May, a ABCNews/Washington Post poll says that the New York tycoon is leading for one point on the Democratic candidate: 46 to 45%. On the other hand, the most wise observers have always warned about enthusiasm - at least premature - sprouted on double digits advantages of the past weeks. Imagine now, that FBI Director James Comey announced to Congress the reopening of Emailgate after having found new emails of the former Secretary of State Hillary Rodham Clinton on Antony Weiner computer, former Democratic politician and almost ex-husband of the right arm of Clinton – Huma Abedin – he too under investigation for having molested several women, including a fifteen-year old, by sending them some pictures of his genitals.

But, why re-open the investigation during the election

campaign for some e-mails whose contents are unknown? For such a simple reason that moved to the background, namely that those e-mails were on the computer of a person like Weiner, which certifies the principle on which the entire accusatory system is built, that is, by using her private mail server, Clinton has endangered the entire US security system.

In short, adding this scandal to a relaxed management of the Clinton Foundation and the experience sometimes disastrous (see ISIS and Benghazi) as Secretary of State, we understand why the game with the crazy variable Trump is far from closed. At this point, if on one hand Hillary Clinton's manager campaign, Robby Mook, tries to refute declaring to CNN that «FBI should publish the material that has gathered about connection between Trump and Russia», on the other hand the Republican candidate, during a meeting in Wisconsin, has invited «all Democratic voters that in Michigan, Pennsylvania and Minnesota have already voted for Hillary Clinton, to change their vote», something that they can actually do by going to the polling station on the election day.

This is something that will mark the passage of time from here up to the election day, a neck and neck which has become exhausting and that, as shown by the poll of the Los Angeles Times, has never ceased to be so. The most interesting elements emerging from the survey of the authoritative California newspaper are essentially two: the fact that Trump has always been ahead of Hillary, and that his advantage is inversely proportional to the degree of education of those interviewed, proving that we too often tend to underestimate the discontent of the so-called silent majority and that, at the end, what counts is always the concept of "one person, one vote".

XIV

FEAR AT TRUMP MEETING
ONE MAN ARRESTED
Vanity Fair - November 6th, 2016

PEOPLE TALK of assassination attempt, but there is no gun. Donald Trump taken away by force by Secret Service agents, scenes of chaos right next to the stage where he was holding a speech in front of his supporters in Reno, Nevada, and a man under arrest.

Trump was in the middle of his speech when the hustle broke out; a man begins to question him, his supporters intervened, with jostling and insults. A glance at the crowd in front of him, annoyed from the spotlight he covers his eyes with one hand and, at that precise moment, the arrival of the agents.

Later a spokesman for the Secret Service stated that «an unidentified individual» shouted «gun» in the crowd even if «after a careful search» no weapon was found. The suspect was immediately taken into custody and taken to a room next to the stage by a group of agents and SWAT officers armed with assault rifles, but at the moment any further details do not leak out except that «an investigation is ongoing».

A matter of minutes, and Trump reappears on stage «nobody can never stop me, I can never thank enough the secret services, they are truly amazing, but now let's go back to what we were saying», he said, before ending his speech.

When the meeting ended, the blond New Yorker tycoon, with an official statement, thanked the agents again and «the thousands of Americans who were there giving their fantastic support», while the social media manager of Trump, Dan Scavino Jr, and Donald Trump Jr, the eldest son of the candidate, have decided to propose a tweet of a certain Jack Posobiec, a supporter who wrote: «Hillary (Clinton) ran away from the rain, instead Trump is back on stage a few minutes after having undergone an assassination attempt».

Pity that the Secret Service statement has clarified that, fortunately, no weapon has been found.

During the campaign of Trump, other two very similar situations have occurred. The first one in March, in Daytona, when Secret Service agents rushed to protect him from a man who wanted to go on stage, and the second one in June in Las Vegas, where a madman tried to steal the gun of a police officer, saying that he wanted to use it «to shoot Trump».

XV

Emailgate, FBI closes
Investigation about Hillary
Vanity Fair - November 7th, 2016

Emailgate, game over. In a letter to the Congress, FBI Director James Comey retracted the sword of Damocles that was hanging on the head of Clinton, defusing in fact, the only weapon at the disposal of Trump who, not by chance, defines the Democratic candidate as crooked, just leveraging the scandal of emails. «On the basis of foregoing investigations, we decided not to change the results stated in July regarding Secretary Clinton», the passage of the letter with which Comey has finally revealed what was certainly the most grey area about the person of Hillary.

«We take note with pleasure that FBI has confirmed the conclusions which she had already made in July», Jennifer Palmieri, head of Clinton staff communication, said with a hint of sarcasm, and then she suddenly changed expression: «I have to make an announcement» she said with a hint of a smile «in Philadelphia we will have a new guest, Bruce Springsteen», flooring all the people on the plane that Hillary uses for the countless displacements of the final rush of her campaign.

The event – at which I will attend for Vanity Fair – will begin on Monday when in Italy it will be approximately 2 am, and it will take place in a charming location such as Independence Hall, which is the building where, on July 4th, 1776, the Founding Fathers ratified the Declaration of Independence, formalizing the birth of the United States of America. Along with Hillary, besides the Boss, on stage there will be another popular rock star, John Bon Jovi, and then

Michelle and Barack Obama, her husband Bill and her daughter Chelsea.

Last October, in an interview with Channel 4 News, Springsteen had described Trump as «a threat to democracy» and then, referring to accusations of manipulated elections said by the Republican candidate, he added that «he knows he will lose, but he is so narcissistic to the point of wanting to dig the dirt on the entire democratic system. If only he would think about what he's doing, but he is not a reflective person. Simply he has no sense of decency, nor is able to assume his responsibility for what he says».

Meanwhile, the campaign manager of Trump, Kellyanne Conway, had first criticized FBI director «I have always said that he mishandled the investigation» and then she went on, stating that «to the Congress, Comey said that Clinton behavior was so irresponsible, jeopardizing national security. This is just one of the reasons why Hillary is not able to inspiring confidence to Americans».

It is certain that quantifying at this moment how much will weigh, in electoral terms, the resolution of the Emailgate scandal, is truly a difficult task, also because, from both sides, many Americans admit they have already decided long ago for whom they will vote, although they do not intend to tell it.

The fact remains that the latest polls keep on saying that Hillary Clinton is ahead in some of the so-called swing states, confirming a significant head to head. The *tracking poll* of Survey Monkey, for instance, sets 262 electoral votes to Clinton and 179 to Trump, while 97 are still hanging in the balance. This means that Hillary has a significant advantage, but it does not mean that the match is already closed. At this stage one thing is certain, that is on Tuesday we will know if the diffidence towards Hillary is a genuine feeling and really widespread among the so-called silent majority or not, and the best thing is that Americans, not surveys nor FBI, will tell it to us.

XVI

THE TRUMP POWER
Vanity Fair - November 9th, 2016

THE STEP from The Apprentice to the White House seemed impossible, yet he, Donald Trump, has done it. Whether you like him or not, in his triumphant ride there is the whole essence of the American Dream: first the victory of the Republican primaries, taking advantage of GOP divisions, and blowing cunningly on the discontent fire, which was burning under the ashes in wait for flaring up once the wind had lifted. Then elections, the real ones. «It is technically impossible he wins», the majority said unwisely, even at our latitudes, although they were still licking their wounds for Brexit. But here he is, The Donald, smiting Hillary, the most unfit candidate that the Democrats could choose. Here at the Jacob Javits Center in New York, which is hosting the Election Night of Hillary Clinton, the atmosphere was immediately surreal, from the beginning it was clear that things were not as everyone had been expected. Serious faces, sealed lips and the obvious embarrassment in the sentences of circumstance with which politicians and staff members answered the reporters who came here from every part of the world. Let's wait, let's see, it's too early.

Meanwhile, on the video walls, one after another, more and more States began to be colored in red. Not only the republican strongholds, but also the so-called *swing states:* Ohio, Florida and even Pensilvania, where only last night, beside Hillary, Bon Jovi, Springsteen, Barack and Michelle Obama have taken it in turns. All in vain, in fact the silent majority, in spite of the polls, went to vote for the New York tycoon, demonstrating how the endorsements are not important, whether they come from star system celebrity, or from a charismatic president like Obama, or from newspapers too. It is a principle which is also true on the contrary, considering that most of the "Colonels" of the Republican Party has publicly distanced itself from the unwelcome frontrunner.

Paradoxically, the fact of having everybody against, played in favor of Trump, who, being a clever and astute communicator, has thought to turn the enemy's fire, and above all the friendly one, into a flag behind which to close ranks of his supporters. «They are against me because I am not one of them, I'm not part of the system. I am your voice», he said in his speech at the Republican Convention that was held in Cleveland last July. A powerful message, which evidently took root.

On the opposite front, in such a context, Hillary has paid the price of what, some time ago, would have been effectively an added value: her experience. How many times have we heard in this election campaign saying «she is the most experienced candidate»? So many times, almost always. Leaving aside scandals, in all likelihood, her path, in a historical moment like the present one, has been perceived by the Americans as the certificate of her belonging to the unpopular establishment.

Of course, saying that anyone else in her place would have beaten Trump is self-evident, as well as unnecessary, because the genuine news of this historical November 8th of 2016 is that, while the curtain falls on Obama experience, trumpism comes to life. It goes without saying that, from now on, the parallels with the two decades of Berlusconi will be countless, but the main difference is that Berlusconi has a personal party, while Trump has not. Now the hope is that Republicans, who won both Congress and Senate, have the will and the strength to counterbalance him.

XVII

TRUMP, THE VICTORY OF AMERICANS
AGAINST THE POWER
Il GiornaleOFF - November 10th, 2016

DONALD TRUMP has never impressed me: too much Nixon and too little Reagan or Coolidge, for my liking. Politically speaking, what I mean. Only then there come issues related to his very deliberately over the top personality, the gossips and all the rest, of which, honestly, I do not care.

I say this few hours after his landmark victory, which I have experienced first hand from the headquarters of his rival at the Javits Center in New York and, above all, after having followed him since his descent into the field for the Republican primaries, and going to Cleveland for the Convention of the Grand Old Party which gave him the same nomination for which I have also "ran" with my fake candidacy, under the false guise of Alex Anderson.

All this has meant that, during the last year, I could exchange views with an indefinite number of Americans of every creed, color and social class. I interviewed some of them, others I met them in informal circumstances, and I met many others – more than 28.000 – through Alex's Twitter profile that, up to the moment I decided to come to the fore, was perceived as a real politician who, unlike the others, used to answer (and still answers) to anyone writing him. Many of them are Republicans and supporters of Trump, the *deplorables*, as they like to define themselves, since Hillary committed one of her many gaffes calling them in this way. I believe, therefore, to say that I have seen at first hand people that the new American president has managed to build around himself, perceiving in an unequivocal way the aversion they have towards the so-called establishment, the apparatus that in the clumsy attempt to delegitimize him, has instead entitled him, making him a real alternative. In the first place, Republicans, torn by personal interests and unable to express a project, even before a credible candidacy. Then Hillary Clinton, at the same time the worst candidate for the Democrats and the best opponent for Republicans.

The Donald saw the gap and has played all out slipping into it and, day after day, provocation after provocation, turning it into the highway that led him straight to the White House.

Endorsements, the almost total adversity of the mainstream media, the bizarre surveys. Totally useless, because it is too distant from the reality of people in the flesh, who can not eat with the big words and the appeals of the stars. Whether you like it or not, in this case we can apply the same principle as of the "level" of Toto: in the voting booth, as well as in front of death, there is no millionaire or poor sod, we are all equal. One person, one vote.

The landmark victory of Donald Trump is the red pill to be swallowed by all those who believed that Hillary Rodham Clinton had to win absolutely, throwing them outside Matrix and catapulting them into the real world. An exceptional challenge, no doubt, which, however, will now have to follow exceptional facts. Only then the masterpiece of Trump will be accomplished.

XVIII

«It is easier to forgive Trump rather than Hillary's lies»
Vanity Fair - November 14th, 2016

LOOKING at it today, it seems that the massive presence of Christopher Columbus statue in front of Trump International Hotel & Tower makes sense, it seems is there to say «yes, it's here» to the tens of thousands of people who, every day, peek out under its most important buildings. The Trump Tower on Fifth Avenue is this, precisely. Just here we meet Cathy, an effervescent model and PR of Staten Island, who during the electoral campaign, has supported Donald Trump with conviction, in spite of his old-fashioned machismo.

30 years old, charming smile and determined manner, Cathy agrees to be interviewed by me without showing the slightest hesitation to stand up for it, quite the contrary. «A lot of friends and people I know disagree with him, but I believe that Trump was the only possibility of change we had», she begins, underlining the fact she attends «many democrats» but she believes in «the values of conservatives».

Cathy starts from afar, from September 11 which in some way is the West's Apocalypse and which, here in New York, after 15 years, still paints expressions of deep sorrow on the face of anyone who speaks about it. «Those living here feel to be the number one target of terrorism and, like many other Americans, I am convinced that President Trump will defend us from this threat», also and above all dealing with immigration, as indeed he has confirmed in the interview given to CBS, in which he insisted that after having built a wall «in order to strengthen the border with Mexico», he will proceed with the expulsion or the imprisonment of «about three million people living illegally in the United States and who are usual to commit criminal acts».

Even for Cathy the fight against illegal immigration is the predominant part of the ground where the victory of Trump has its roots, because «this is a country which was born from immigration, and no one is against immigrants a priori», but one thing is who comes here «to work honestly, integrating himself and paying taxes» but something very different are those «who come to the United States illegally, and have no intention to normalize their position because they live clandestinity the same way as a twilight zone where it is easier to commit a crime».

As for the dream to see a woman into the Oval Office, according to Cathy it has been shattered by the Democrats «in the very moment when they agreed to undergo the candidacy of Hillary Clinton» who, in her opinion, could never have won because «for us Americans the sincerity of a person is crucial, and it is much easier to ignore some trivialities of Trump, rather than the huge lies like those of Clinton», like the ones concerning «Emailgate and Clinton Foundation», with which the former First Lady would «jeopardized national security for reasons which are not completely understood yet».

Just as our conversation comes to an end, a woman who in all likelihood had taken part in anti-Trump event a few hours before from Union Square, began to scream out loud a few sentences against the new president: that was enough to make a dozen police cars appeared immediately. Document control, an invitation to stop, and that's it, all over. Police cars disappear again into the darkness that has in the meantime wrapped Manhattan and, after greeting me, Cathy walks away briskly toward the Madison Square Garden, also disappearing into the horizon composed of a multitude of colored lights and people, each with their own ideas, problems, fears and dreams, but with the certainty that, as

Obama said on election night, yes, «the sun will rise again tomorrow».

XIX

WE WALKED INTO THE HEADQUARTERS
OF TRUMP. THIS IS WHAT WE FOUND
Facebook webpage Elezioni USA 2016
November 14th, 2016

SOON, just a couple of kilometers away, it would take place the last big event of the electoral campaign of Hillary Clinton: John Bon Jovi, Bruce Spingsteen, Barack and Michelle Obama, Bill and Chelsea Clinton, a charming and significant locations such as the Independence Mall, and an audience of over 30,000 people. But first, I decided to go and visit the Republican General Headquarters in Pennsylvania in order to figure out how they were organized and what kind of atmosphere there was over there.

As soon as I reached my destination, I immediately felt there was something wrong. Yes, well, I thought, is not it possible this is the headquarters of the electoral campaign of Trump in a key state like Pennsylvania!

As I crossed the threshold, I found myself in a tiny office where four people, packed, were working. Two men in their sixties, a younger one, Dan, introduced himself as the organizational manager, and Susan, a middle-aged woman, welcomed me at the door.

«Good morning, can we help you?», she asked me very warmly. Immediately I tried to break the ice introducing myself as a freelance reporter but, as soon as they told me the press was not allowed, I decided to play Alex Anderson card. So, I pulled out some pins from my backpack and, when they realized who I was, instantly they changed their attitude, inviting me to sit down and giving me a cup of steaming coffee.

«How are you organized for the last few hours of this electoral campaign? Honestly I thought to find much more people», I asked them. «We have many volunteers who are making the last phone calls, but we believe we have done such a great job, and that tomorrow night Hillary will have to swallow a very bitter pill», Dan replied, while Susan, after having fixed the pin of Alex on the lapel of her jacket, brought me some bumper stickers and some of their flyers.

«Trump does not need to spend the millions which Hillary is investing to beat her, he will win because it is on the side of people», she said, pointing the street «You see, there's lots of people out there who no longer has a job or, if he has one, is struggling to put together the money to pay rent and bills. The whole working class will vote for him», she went on, before throwing her things randomly in her bag, and greet me with a «see you Alex, take care» and leaving the office.

«Hillary is rotten and corrupt, people do not want her, not because she is a woman, but because she is cynical and merciless», said the man who used to sit glued to the wall on which the logo Trump–Pence was.

At that point I asked if I could shoot a video but, after they told me it was not possible because «we have already given you a great opportunity allowing you to stay here», I asked if I could take some pictures at least. Dan nodded, reluctantly, but he nodded. So I took photographs to what you are watching on this post: forms, blackboard, posters pro Trump and those against Hillary. If there was the mimeograph too, then it would have been like being in the ramshackle headquarters of a circle of a suburban party circle, twenty or thirty years ago.

Perhaps, one of the most romantic aspects of this tremendous electoral campaign, has been only that, namely,

David Trump won against Goliath Clinton and all her immeasurable deployment of spin doctor, show business stars, media and so on. For a full package, probably it only lacked the endorsement of Mickey Mouse and Donald Duck.

Taking it too into consideration, anyone who has a minimum of intellectual honesty, can not but admit that the campaign of Trump, starting from the Republican primaries, has been absolutely extraordinary. Now that we have known the qualities of the candidate Trump, we expect to see the ones of president Trump, in the hope that his work is up to his talk.

XX

«WE, THE TRUMP'S PEOPLE»
Vanity Fair - January 24th, 2017

UNLIKE what you could imagine, "People of Trump" is made up of Americans of all origins and social class who, in last days, have crowded the streets of Washington creating what we could easily define the Trump Pride. A veritable army which followed its leader without worrying too much about either the incidents occurred just after the Inauguration Day on Friday, and either the Womens March on Saturday, because «that's people who love democracy only when their candidates win», said Peter, who defines himself «one of the few Republicans who supported Trump since the very beginning», to whom his wife Christine immediately makes echo, wearing a shimmering dress with sequins making up the mosaic of the American flag, adding that «to sermonise against Trump, there were people like Madonna, who promised oral sex to all men who would have voted for Hillary. A shame».

But now, however, let's go back and live together these three days.

January 18th

It's seven pm and, as soon as I reach the hotel, I go out for a walk to enjoy the atmosphere of the city which is almost ready for the big event; at this hour Pennsylvania Avenue is a bustle of people leaving offices and hastening toward house. I decide to take a walk towards the White House, where they are working hard for the Inauguration Day on Friday: metal grandstands on both sides of the roads, cockades and flags hung everywhere, and crowds of Trump supporters chasing the right glimpse in order to be able to take a selfie. «Obama has been a true disaster and Hillary would have been a tragedy, thank God who won is the candidate who will sweep away all the shit from Washington», George tells me, a giant of about two meters just arrived from Texas. My last conversation of the day is with Michael, the Uber driver who, at the end of the journey to the hotel, dismisses me with an apparently obvious concept, but which in reality is the essence of this extraordinary Country, namely that the victory of Trump «is the demonstration that everything is truly possible in America».

January 19th

«Someone will try to kill him», Will tells me with certainty, an old black waiter who makes no secret about the fact he «voted for Trump because he is against state powers, he bothers, that's why they are wearing him out». After breakfast, I decide to have a walk up to the Capitol, a path along which the historic event takes shade: hawkers displaying their goods strictly branded Trump, soldiers and police officers scattered everywhere (there are 28,000 units), journalists at every street corners broadcasting live through their smartphones, but also a group of homeless people whose only interest is to be warmed by the hot steam rising from a grid. When I reach the foot of the Capitol, I stay for over half an hour to contemplate the stage from where 55 years ago John F. Kennedy uttered the famous speech of «do not ask what your country can do for you, ask yourself what you can do for your country». I write some notes and then I move on towards the National Mall, where in a couple of hours the "Make America Great Again Concert" will start. After a discrete queue at the entrance exclusively for the press, I go into the park which, between the Washington Monument and the Lincoln Memorial, gives way to the Reflecting Pool, on whose sides tens of thousands of people take place singing loudly every single note of "Proud to be an

American" sung by country singer Lee Greenwood and who go into ecstasies when Donald Trump and his wife Melania make their entrance on stage.

January 20th

Here at the Mall, there are so many people and you can perceive the atmosphere of an appointment with history, at which nevertheless is good to take part, just even to say «I was there». With the passage of minutes the atmosphere is getting warmer and, when on the videowalls Hillary Clinton's face appears, someone shouts «arrest her!». Among the multitude of red hats and Trump flags, there are also cartels of those who accuses him of racism and servility towards Putin. Supporters of President watch, sometimes comment, but they let it slide. «It's the first time I come to Washington and I did it just for him», an old supporter of Trump says, just arrived from Illinois with his wife. According to Lisa, Californian of 28 year old, «is a change, finally in the direction of people. I'm very happy», while her friend Courtney has a different opinion, believing that «we will regret Obama very soon». In the meanwhile, under a gray sky, raindrops start falling just when Donald Trump begins to speak. The evangelical pastor Franklin Graham, who spoke just after him, says that it is a good omen because «in the Bible, the rain is a sign of God's blessing».

XXI

THE 5 ELEMENTS WHICH MADE TRUMP WIN

by Francesco Fabiano

IT IS CERTAINLY easier make an examination of the winning features of a candidate after his victory. Actually, we've been focused on these 5 winning features of Donald Trump, since long time ago, through studies and analysis carried out by the professional team of Politic Manager, which now we propose you:

I - ENERGY
The powerful physical presence, which could even be a boomcrang, was used in an effective manner especially through self-control of the body through slow and continuous movements of his walk. By contrast, the use of gestures was characterized by blunt and sudden movements of the hands and by a very empathetic facial mimicry which often emphasized the concepts even taking them to the extreme with clear strong facial expressions, revealing of specific emotions and coherent with the person. His body was controlled, but gestures and facial expressions were free to convey strong feelings, explosive energy and courage to express his true emotions.

II - INDIPENDENCE
The constant references to his story of successful businessman or to his own career as a public and media personality, have done nothing but widen the concept of "winning experiences of life" of Donald Trump. Even his "extended" family was lived by him and presented to people as something normal, pointing to a significant "management" skills of people and complex and conflicting life affairs. His

story as a man first Republican, then supporter for democrats for a few years, and then as an independent front-runner "against" both sides (until almost the end of the run) has communicated independence and mental flexibility. Ability to make, concretely, assessments and choices without bias. The fact of being unpopular, mocked and attacked by the entire political, economical, cultural and mass media establishment, did the rest.

III - CHANGE

Donald Trump was not afraid to use "politically incorrect" expressions, unpublished and original sentences, judgments and observations, with respect to the existing panorama of political communication. The change has been embodied and communicated effectively mainly through language. A simple and direct syntax. Short and incisive sentences. Positions (sometimes even risky and questionable) expressed in a clear and sharp way with a confident unmistakable tone. Very far away from the political jargon and radically different from the cautious and equidistant diplomatic language of the economical/technocratic establishment, which is often perceived as empty, repetitive and cloying.

IV - COURAGE

The initial choice to present himself as independent with respect to any factions and autonomous with respect to the great centers of economical and media power, has shown to all Americans, what, in my opinion, has been the most insightful and decisive feature among all those shown. Ezra Pound used to say *" If a man is not willing to fight for his ideas, or his ideas are worth nothing, or he is worthless"*. The courage of Trump was to believe and to carry on, with undoubted courage, ideas and proposals which initially were outside the great political debate on the media, but were well-rooted and present in large part of the American society and population.

V - VIRILITY

It was since Ronald Reagan period, the Cowboy, that you could not see a "male" candidate as Trump. His definitely masculine connotation, in contrast with most refined candidates (like Romney) or more empathetic (like Obama) was used and communicated in order to embody a veritable fatherly figure of the nation. A father, even harsh and authoritarian, but sincere, loyal and able to pass down, through his virility, a remarkable capability of being a determined and authoritative leader. On the other hand, a candidate who has not been able to express all the wide and rich range of female connotations, has done the rest.

Links:

Alessandro Nardone on Twitter:
https://www.twitter.com/alenardone

Alessandro Nardone on Facebook:
https://www.facebook.com/alessandronardone

Alessandro Nardone on Youtube:
https://www.youtube.com/alenardone

Alex Anderson on Twitter:
https://www.twitter.com/americaisnow

Alessandro Nardone's website:
https://www.alexanderson.biz

Alex Anderson's campaign website:
https://www.alexanderson2016.com

Francesco Fabiano's website:
https://www.francescofabiano.com

Politic Manager:
https://www.politicmanager.com

*My thanks go to you, Vittoria:
you are and you will always be my greatest success!*

Dad

Printed in February 2019
by Youcanprint Self-Publishing